W9-ANN-357

To the person who reads this book,
I pray this book will serve you where
you need it most!

Keep Moving Forward

Sean Wyman

LET GO

The Movement Process

~Sean Wyman~

Let Go: The Movement Process

© 2016 Sean Wyman

Contact me directly@

successwithseanwyman@gmail.com

Let's be Social @:

https://www.facebook.com/successwithsean

https://www.facebook.com/successwithseanwyman/

https://twitter.com/successwithsean

https://www.linkedin.com/in/successwithseanwyman

https://www.instagram.com/successwithseanwyman/

https://www.periscope.tv/successwithseanwyman

For great success strategies check out my website @

http://www.successwithseanwyman.com/

Check out the Success Movement Radio Show

http://successmovementradio.com/

Published in the United States of America

To my mother,

Thank you for everything you gave up and went through for me. It took years to realize what you had really done. All those years I thought you had given me up at the age of 10 because you did not want me in your life. Now I understand that what you did saved my life. Because of your sacrifice, I have been able to live a life filled with God's purpose, have an amazing family, and help others to eliminate their self-doubt and find their purpose in life. I am honored to dedicate this book to you.

forgiveness

Acknowledgements

Special thank you to Lynn, Orian, Timmy, and Shalyn Your support means everything to me!

I would also like to thank the following people for inspiring me to do this:

Lauretta Pierce

James MacNeil

Desiree Lee

Adam Flores

Ken Loring

Table of Contents

Introduction

I believe everyone should be able to live a purpose-driven life that allows them to be in control. The problem is a lot of people want to live a life full of purpose and meaning but they get hung up on fear and self-doubt from things that have occurred in the past.

I used to be the same way. As someone who grew up in a challenging childhood, made a lot of mistakes along the way, and faced adversity as a Police Officer, Military Veteran, Father, Husband, and Entrepreneur, I understand how people allow things from the past to get in the way of their future.

It was not until I learned how to create MOVEMENT that my life changed, and it will

What does this mean?

never be the same. When I discovered there was a process I went through to deal with my challenging past that allowed me to progress to my future, I knew I had to write this book to serve others who needed help doing the exact same thing.

Now as we get started on this journey together, my goal is to lay out this process so as soon as you get done reading this book you can discover how to let go of your past and create MOVEMENT in your life.

Consider this your self-help guide to help you eliminate your self-doubt and fear from the past, and move forward with your life. So as we get started together I want to be the first to say Welcome to the Movement!

Foreword by Author
James MacNeil

Congratulations for caring enough about your life, and the impact your life will undoubtedly have on others' lives, to invest yourself in this book. I encourage you to dive in head, and heart, first. Allow yourself to be affected by the stories, principles, and insights found herein. Plan to take appropriate action with all you will glean from this powerful and heart-rich book. Sean Wyman is truly one in a billion and this book is too!

I have been blessed with the opportunity to work with, speak with, and on occasion, do business with, some of the world's most powerful, influential, and wealthy individuals. I'm grateful for these opportunities and I'm grateful for all that I've learned from these unique and wonderful people. With this in mind it may come as a surprise that I have not met many people I would refer to as my hero, but Sean Wyman is my hero!

Comic books and Hollywood scripts love to touch our hearts with tales of unique individuals who have been crushed by the brutal effects of great loss and treachery. The difference between heroes and victims is clear as these heroes, may initially appear to be victims, but only for a season because they have that special something, which we all long to experience, that special something that does not quit, does not resign itself to destruction or justified excuses, but somehow, beyond all reasonable expectation, breaths again, and stirs again, and rises again, heals and strengthens and becomes, as a result of this brutal experience, bigger, stronger, faster, kinder, gentler, braver, and they turn their personal tragedy into their preparatory tomb from which they emerge our hero.

Sean Wyman in a real life sense is one of these heroes, but he has gone one massive step farther than any marvel comic character. Sean has systematized his secrets to surviving and thriving and turning tragedy into triumph. Sean reveals in these pages his step-by-step formula to manage life, including its toughest twists, and to harness

14

your life experiences to realize your best possible, purpose-driven, life.

I encourage you to allow The MOVEMENT to ignite the action-taking hero in you.

James MacNeil
Author and Founder of Verbal Aikido
Pure Communication Mastery

Chapter 1

Since the Day I Was Born

Isn't our son beautiful Gary? Yeah, Sean is a beautiful child but I gotta be honest with you Janice, I was not planning on having a child this early in life. I want to be with you but I am not ready for kids yet. Hey, would you be open to putting Sean up for adoption? I mean we are so young and I want to have kids but just not right now. We can build on our relationship and then later on when we're ready we can have kids of our own?

That's how I imagined that conversation went May 4, 1972, in Clearwater Florida when my father told my mother that he didn't want to have a child at that time and left. Luckily for me, my mom chose me over my father. Since the day I was born adversity came into my life. Of course, I did not know I had adversity in my life at the time but it was there. Maybe some of you can relate to adversity that you had in your life at some time or another. If the answer is yes, then you are in the right place because I am going to share some of my adversarial times. I am also going to share the process I discovered through my life that moved me to share my story to help you through your adversity.

After my mother and father split up we moved out west. My mother took me to my grandparents' in Wyoming while she was going to school and focusing on becoming a nurse. I don't remember a whole lot about my grandparents because I was so young but my mom used to tell me about my grandfather and how successful he was as a businessman with Texaco oil company. My grandparents would watch me while my mom was out studying and going to school and doing the things she needed to do to make sure that we had a good life. They used to love taking me out on the boat. In the back of the house, they had this beautiful lake and they would spend hours with me on the boat because I loved it so much. My grandparents created a great bond with me.

Unfortunately, at some point adversity struck again. My grandparents decided that I would be better off being raised by them then by my mother. I don't know the exact circumstances that made this happen but I do know that my mom fought for me. My mom explained to me she had to go through a very challenging lawsuit because my grandparents were so wealthy and successful.

When it was all said and done and the dust settled my mom won custody of me. Unfortunately, my mom lost the relationship with her mom, whom she loved very much.

After the incident with my grandparents, we moved to Albuquerque, New Mexico, where my mom continued her education and graduated and became a nurse. All the way through my seventh year I remember having amazing memories. One of my favorites was when my mom and I went to church on Sundays and then we would just go spend time together. As crazy as it sounds, one of my most favorite times was when she took me to go see the original Star Wars. I loved the time that I had with my mother over the first seven years of my life.

That all came to an end though when my mom met the love of her life. I will never forget how happy she was. She smiled from ear-to-ear, had nothing but great things to say, and fell head over heels in love with this guy. To me, it seemed to happen so fast. Soon after they met my mom went to Washington DC for a week. When she returned she told me we were moving to Washington DC. She said Thomas was a very successful businessman. She was so excited as she was telling me all of the wonderful experiences we were going to have and the amazing life that we were going to live. She shared with me how this man was so excited about spending the rest of his life with us and raising me as his own son. Of course, that got me excited and soon after we drove from Albuquerque, New Mexico, all the way to Washington DC. It was such a fun trip.

It wasn't long after we got to Washington DC that we discovered our dream had become a nightmare. Soon after we arrived, we found out that my new stepfather was indeed a businessman, but not the successful businessman he had made himself out to be. He was a businessman of the street. He was a hustler and a street survivor. He was a drug dealer and a drug user. We lived in a crack-infested neighborhood in Seat Pleasant, Maryland. We had no running water and no electricity for a long time. I remember going and stealing water from our neighbors next door so we could bathe and flush the toilet. We did not celebrate birthdays and holidays because we just could not afford to. To eat we stole from convenience stores and we lived off of the McDonald's Value Menu. To this day I will not touch a Big Mac. My stepfather taught me how to

22

survive. I was taught to steal, panhandled at grocery stores for change, and learned to survive on the street.

As a year went by, I watched my stepfather take the strongest woman I knew and make her weak. I remember the worst nights, watching him mentally and physically abuse her right in front of me. He would ridicule her, mentally demean her, and physically hit her. I felt so helpless. I was too young and afraid to stop him. I will never forget my first physical encounter with Thomas. I had come home from a friend's house and was late for dinner. My friend's parents called and told my stepfather what had happened and asked that I be allowed to stay and eat.

My stepfather hesitantly agreed. When I got home my stepfather greeted me as I came to the front door. He escorted me to the back yard. We sat in the backyard and he told me how hard-headed little boys have to listen to their parents. We were having this conversation when all of the sudden, out of the pitch black darkness, he sucker punched me right in the face. I fell backward off of my seat and my head slammed against the ground. At eight years old, I took my first real punch.

Thomas was no small man. He was well over 6 foot tall and weighed about 250lbs. When he hit me it was square in the nose and tears welled up as I fell backward. I did not know what had just happened. I was shocked. I remember him telling me, "You better dry it up before we go inside, and don't say anything to your mother." As I walked in the door with tears streaming down my face and my mother saw me. Of course, she immediately asked me what happened. I told her that Thomas had just punched me. She looked at me in disbelief and asked, "What did you just say?" As he walked in the door, my mom and Thomas got into a physical confrontation right in front of me.

Over the next two years, I was mentally and physically abused on a regular basis. My mom worked as a nurse at a nursing home. I always wondered where her money went. Only years later did I learn that a large portion went to my stepfather's drug habit. Thomas was addicted to heroin and cocaine. Thomas was meanest when he was not high. Those times, I took some serious beatings. I got hit with everything you could think of, given that his weapon of choice was whatever was in arm's reach: metal rakes, hatchets, belts, cut pine wood slabs, tools, you name it. He had so much rage and anger inside of him. I would find out later his issues were related to back pain and the medicine he was provided was a major part of his issues. The most minor thing could set him off into an uncontrollable rage.

The drugs he took would balance things out and allow him to manage the pain. When he became the angriest, he would bite down on his lower lip and scrunch his eyes. I became conditioned to know when that look showed up I was in for a beating.

I ran away from home three times. Each time the police caught me and brought me home. This would, of course, lead to another beating. At school, the teachers saw the bruises and reported the incidents, but nothing ever happened.

Growing up in a predominantly poor African American suburb environment was awful. This was the first time in my life I was exposed to racism. My stepfather was African American and my mom was white. Living in this environment I ended up going to a school where there were only three white kids in the whole school including me. I hated school. We were broke, so I wore the same clothes to school every day. I was made fun of, laughed at, and fought every day because I was a white kid that the African American kids did not want around them. My nose was broken at least 5 times that I know of and it was not until recently that I had a surgery to be able to breathe correctly through my nose.

Because I was white I got into fights almost every day. I learned very quickly not to lose fights. The first time I lost one, I came home crying, looking for condolence. What I got instead was another beating. Thomas threw me out of the house and told me to go back and "beat that boy's ass and you better not come home until you do." Needless to say, I learned to fight to survive both the fight and the fight to come if I lost.

Thomas would sell drugs late at night on the street corners in downtown Washington DC. At the time, Washington DC was one of the top murder capitals in the world. I would sit in his truck for hours sitting there watching him sell drugs at the liquor store.

I remember nights peeing in a bottle because he threatened to hurt me if I got out of the truck for any reason. People looking like zombies would come out of nowhere and walk by and look at me in the truck. Then they would go meet with my step father to get hooked up. He was a hustler and he was not ashamed to brag about it. He used to tell me stories all the time about how much smarter he was then everyone else including the police. He would tell me how no cop would mess with him because he would kill them. He would tell me how white people were evil and racist even though both my mother and I were white. The mental and physical abuse continued for the next 2 years.

I cannot tell you how many times my stepfather would tell me "You keep it up, your momma is gonna come home to find you buried in the backyard" and I believed with all my heart this man would kill me if I gave him a reason.

Then one night it almost happened. A school function ran forty-five minutes after it was supposed to, and my step father was furious. He had been sitting in the truck waiting for me to come out. When I got to the truck, he started calling me every name in the book. He went on to say how bad I was, and how I had it coming. As we walked through the front door, it happened. Thomas shoved me up against a wall and started punching me uncontrollably. His arms were flying from the left and the right. Punch after punch I took. He was in a complete rage and out of control. Then he grabbed his belt and started hitting me all over my body. The beating went on well over an hour, until I fell unconscious.

When I woke up, it was day time. The sun was coming in through my window. I was lying in my bed on my back and my mother and Thomas were looking over me. I had been beaten so badly that I could not move. My mother and Thomas were both crying. Thomas said over and over again how sorry he was. My frail ten-year-old body was bruised all over. It hurt to blink, let alone move. I was so angry. It was at this point that I made my plan to escape once and for all. But first I was going to make sure he would never hurt anyone else again. I plotted how I was going to kill him.

When I could walk again, the plan was to shoot him in his sleep and then run away from home. He kept a small pistol in the back left pocket of his jeans. He used to show it to me all the time and talk about how if anyone screwed with him he had something for them. I knew where the gun would be and how to gain access to it. Luckily, even though I did not realize it at the time God was there and I did not go through with that part of my plan. Instead, I packed my bag and ran away from home.

As I reflect back on life, I know now how much God was with me during this time. I was a ten-year-old runaway in downtown Washington D.C., one of the most dangerous cities in the world. Miraculously, I survived for three days on my own. People bought me food, I was able to find shelter in the downtown Marriott, and it was not until I got so tired on the third day and fell asleep in the lobby that I was caught by a hotel security guard. The police called my mom and told her I was safe and that they wanted to bring me home. My mother told them not to bring me home because it was not safe for me to come back.

This started my journey into foster care. From age ten to eighteen, I was in the foster care system. I bounced around from foster homes and group homes until I was around fifteen when I finally settled in with foster parents that really cared for me. I went to 7 different schools between 10 and 15 years old. Because of my time in foster care, I had a very strong work ethics early in my life. My foster parents would always want to buy me the cheapest, ugliest clothes. When I protested, they would say, "When you buy them, you can get what you want." With that, at the age of twelve, I got my first job at a restaurant in Laurel, Maryland. My employer paid me under the table to do all the dirty jobs, from sorting dead crabs from live ones, washing crab pots, and stocking beer coolers. I learned the value of earning money very quickly. I made $100 a week working at this place. Since then, I have worked in several professions from restaurants, shoe stores, construction, and everything in between. My drive was towards the almighty paycheck. I learned that money allowed me to buy the things I wanted.

I also learned the importance of being passionate and appreciative about my work. I have always been a hard worker and passionate about what I do. People notice when you are passionate about your profession, no matter what you do. I believe this had to do with what I endured in Washington D.C. There were several excuses I could have made to not make something of myself. Instead, I chose to learn from the things that happened to me. I flipped a switch in my mind and decided that I would never live the way I did as a child. I vowed to myself that when I had a family of my own, I would make sure they never experienced the things that I had to endure. So many people today make excuses and blame their past for their reason not to create their future.

You have to be willing to set aside your excuses. Jim Rhon said it best when he said:

"Excuses are well made up lies and actions create results. If you want something you will find a way and if you don't you will find an excuse."

I had a lot of people that allowed me to make excuses growing up because of what I had gone through. The truth is you are responsible for your success and failure. The challenges you face in your life will impact you positively and negatively but you are the one that will dictate the actions to take, to move forward towards your success.

After going into foster care I really did not care about school. Part of that may have been because I went through so many schools because of the different foster homes and group homes I was in. Part of it was because I was more interested in drinking, smoking, and experimenting with drugs. I started drinking at 13 years old and was addicted to alcohol over 15 years.

It was not until my junior year of high school that something inside of me clicked and help me to realize I needed to graduate high school. I graduated high school in June of 1990 and thought to myself, "Now I am an adult. I can do what I want.

Chapter 2

Welcome to the Real World

By the time I was fifteen I had made a
decision that I wanted to go into law
enforcement. Police officers were a very positive
thing in my life through some of the most
challenging times. When I ran away Police
Officers were there to make sure I was okay.
When I got in trouble for being in the wrong
place at the wrong time the Police were firm but
understanding. When I was robbed one night at
gun point, working at a pizza place along with my
manager, the police were the ones that showed
up. I had the pleasure of meeting a K9 Handler

through one of the foster homes that I lived at. I would go a few times a week and help him with his retired police dogs and he would share cool experiences he had while on the job. I had police officers that would come check on me and ask me how my grades were. As I grew up I knew this would be my calling one day.

When I graduated high school, I made the decision to go back to Albuquerque, New Mexico. Something inside of me led me to believe that all of the challenges and the painful things I had gone through would just go away if I went back to where I was most happy before it all started. I quickly found out that was not the case. It was difficult finding a job. Because I was only 18, I was not able to apply to become a police officer yet, but I did discover a unique opportunity to get going in the right direction. The Albuquerque

Police Department had a Police Service aide program. The program allowed people who wanted to become police officers in the future to work within the police department supporting police officers by doing the mediocre tasks so police officers could deal with the serious ones. This was the first stepping stone into the law enforcement world even though I would not become a police officer for several more years.

Being a Police Service Aide was such an awesome experience. I wore a baby blue uniform with a badge. I did not carry weapons but I did have a flash light. I drove a white car with orange lights and I got to work with police officers on a daily basis. The more I worked with them the more I wanted to be one of them. I gravitated towards the officers that had military background in the special operations field. These guys stood out in the way they approached situations and dealt with people. I had a great respect for them.

As great as the experience was, the position only paid minimum wage. Living on my own I had to have my own apartment, food, and transportation. For the first couple of years I lived what can only be known as "the ultimate bachelor life" I lived off of ramen noodles, popcorn, and macaroni and cheese to survive. Finally, the time came. I put in about 2 years as a Police Service Aide and had created a good reputation as a hard worker. I submitted my application to become an Albuquerque police officer. I went through the process with no problem. I knew when I walked into the final oral board that this was it. I was getting ready to become a police officer. What I discovered was a panel who did not see a young man who was ready to become a police officer.

Instead they saw a boy who wanted to be a man who was immature, looked young for his age, and needed more time before he was ready.

They asked me to stay on as a Police Service Aide for one more year, go through the process one more time, and I would have a high chance of being selected. I will never forget how angry I was. I looked the panel in the eye and told them they just made the biggest mistake of their life and walked out. I got in my car and I started driving home thinking about how stupid these guys were to not select me. As I drove down the road I looked to my left and there it was the Army recruiting station. I pulled in and an hour later I was enlisted.

There is a valuable lesson to be learned here. I like to call it the check and balances lesson.

Because I was too young and was not ready to be a police officer, my immaturity stood out and by lashing out I proved the panel right. I did not check my ego and balance my emotions because I did not know how. This is one of the most important skills to acquire in your life. The sooner you can check your ego and balance your emotions the better you will be able to see things with clarity and make decisions based on experience and facts. I know now those people were looking out for my best interest along with the police department's best interest.

Going into the military was my first big mental adjustment. The military had it down to a science when it came to making soldiers see their true potential. They showed me that you really are whatever you think you are, and that you can build your mental toughness by demanding more from yourself. Going through all the challenges in the military was a huge part of my transformation. In order to make any change in your life, you have to truly invest in your personal development and not invest in something you don't believe in. Until you invest in yourself you will never be truly invested in yourself.

Confidence was not my strong suit. But when I joined the Army, it forced me to face my fears head on. I had to do things I had never done and face my fears. One of my most significant moments came at my first assignment in Fort Campbell, Kentucky. I decided I wanted to be an Airborne Ranger. Now, at the time I was 5'6" and 120lbs soaking wet. To say this was the most challenging school I had ever attended would be an understatement. At Fort Benning Georgia, I underwent my first true leadership development training. The things I learned there would stay with me for life—a life that almost ended in June 1994.

That summer, we were in the last phase of Ranger School known as the Jungle Phase or "Swamp Phase," trampling around Eglin Air Force Base in Florida. We had just done a rope bridge crossing over the Yellow River. I was carrying approximately 80 pounds in my rucksack with an M-60 machine gun slung in front of me that weighed approximately 26lbs. I had lost weight since I first signed up, and was down to under 112 pounds. When we all got across the river, we started moving out. The point man went off course, and we ended up in a really nasty woodland environment. Every step was a challenge because we were getting tangled up in vines and thick underbrush. Then it happened. I tripped and fell straight forward. The rucksack on my back slammed down with 80 pounds of force on my neck at the base of my spine, while at the same time the weight of the M-60 and a little thing called gravity pulled me to the ground. I could not move. I had pinched a nerve in my neck and was physically paralyzed and terrified.

The Ranger instructors were called over and they were yelling at me. "Get up, Ranger," they said again and again. I tried with all my might, but I could not move. The Ranger instructors realized I was injured and said they had to get me to the hospital. The environment was so thick that the helicopter could not land. They had to make a clearing and called the helicopter in to lower a litter to put me in and lift me up into the helicopter. I remember hearing the helicopter come in. I was laid into the litter. In those days, there was a guideline and an anchor line to keep the litter straight while it was being lifted up. I began to feel my body get light as I came up off the ground. I could see the shadowy outline of the helicopter as I began to rise up towards it.

Suddenly, I heard a loud pop and I started spinning. First slowly, then faster and faster and faster, until I felt like I was going as fast as the helicopter rotors. As it turned out, the guideline had not been put on correctly, and when it brushed what I can only assume was a tree branch, it broke, sending the litter rotating under the helicopter. I spun under the helicopter for approximately 15 minutes. Meanwhile, the gravitational force pushed all the blood up to my head and blew out all the blood vessels in my face. I was terrified. I gripped onto the litter as I felt myself sliding out slowly. I just knew at any second, I was going to plunge to my death. Once again God was there! An experienced pilot, made long banks to slow the litter down to lift me up little by little. I will never forget the moment when they finally got me in the helicopter. I heard a guy say, "If you can hear me, squeeze my hand." I grabbed that hand and squeezed for all I was worth, and then passed out. I woke up hours later in the hospital with nurses making fun of me and complaining about how bad I stunk. I was four days from graduation.

All I could think about was finishing. I did not care about my health or what condition I was in. I just wanted to finish. Before I had left, my Sargent Major made it very clear that he was not pleased I was being allowed to go to Ranger School as a Private First Class. With even more clarity he explained to me the only way I was to come back was with my Ranger tab or dead. Those were the only options. On my third day in the hospital, I convinced the doctors to let me back out. I agreed to sign waivers and accept responsibility for my current condition. I had limited vision in both eyes, and they were bloodshot red. Through my persistence, I got back out with my squad in time for the last day in the field. I faced my fear of dying and turned it into fuel to persevere and finish what I had started. We started out with 420 people and just over 100 of us graduated. I was so proud that I completed Ranger School. It is one of the greatest accomplishments of my life.

I ended up spending eight years in the army. After my near-death experience, I realized that if I would have died I didn't have any legacy to leave behind. That led me to change my thinking. I decided I wanted to get married and have a family.

SAME!!!

SAME

I now realized how short life really was and that tomorrow is promised to none of us. I married my first wife just before I left Fort Campbell Kentucky to go to Italy. Unfortunately, our marriage only lasted for 3 years. Two and a half of those three years I was deployed either in training or real world scenarios. The positive thing that came out of our marriage was my first son.

It's funny how history comes back around at the strangest times. My son had a medical complication when he was born so my wife came back to the United States, where he was born. I was able to come back from Italy on a hardship tour so I could be with them. Shortly after I returned, my wife told me she wanted a divorce. I was devastated. Here we had a beautiful child and I believed in my heart that we could make things work. She had already made up her mind though, so I had a very challenging decision to make.

My reenlistment was coming up and I had to make a decision to stay in the army and continue my career or to get out and start a new one. Because my father had left me when I was born the decision was easy. I got out and started my law enforcement career. I'm proud to say that was a great decision and I'm honored that I've had the opportunity to be in my son's life over the last 18 years.

Chad Read this ↓

One of my biggest regrets was my divorce. It devastated me mentally and physically. I ended up over $90,000 Dollars in debt not including over $100,000 in child support. The relationship after the fact was volatile and very difficult and it was obvious we did not have the same ideas on what

50

we wanted from life and wanted for our son's life. It was really frustrating for me, because this was not how I pictured my life at the age of 26. I had been raised that marriage was sacred and it was a very difficult time for me. Finally, I realized if I was going to be a good father to my son I had to let go and focus on what I could control and not what I could not. God had another plan for me. I just did not realize it yet!

I went into the military because I wanted the skills to be a good police officer and that is exactly what I got. I did everything I wanted to do in law enforcement from a Patrol Officer, Vice Narcotics Investigator, Community Police Officer, Field Training Officer, K9 Handler, and even a Tactical Entry Team Operator on our SWAT Team that we called Tactical Apprehension and Control Team. Everything I ever wanted to do in my childhood dreams I accomplished.

Now I want to show you that no matter what you've gone through in your life, what adversity you faced, or what challenges you have had to go through you can let go and create movement to change the things in your life that you want to change and move forward. You may be asking yourself, "how is this possible?" It's okay to say it. I know I did. The answer is by implementing the 8 step movement process I am going to share with you. Ready to get started?

Chapter 3

Victims, Survivors, and Winners

As I faced the challenges of being abused, almost dying, and going through an ugly divorce, I went through a process. In this chapter I am going to share with you what I discovered along my journey of letting go, adapting, healing, and overcoming all these events and more importantly how you can too. I believe there are three stages that I went through, and each stage was very important. As you read this, if you are currently going through a challenging situation this will help you identify where you are at and what to strive towards in the future.

When I first started out I was the victim. The victim is the first stage and it is a very vulnerable stage. Let's face it, the victim stage is rough. This is the stage where you are trying to figure everything out. Was it my fault? What did I do to deserve this? What is wrong with me? These were all questions that came to mind for me. The victim does not trust easily. After all the trust has been broken multiple times before most even realize they are the victim. I remember having this "us against them mentality". I blamed everyone for my problems and I was never wrong. No one else could understand my pain because they had not been there. At least that was what went through my mind.

The truth though is a lot of people can relate to you and have felt your pain or worse, but during the victim stage you are your top priority.

Another challenge victims face is letting go of the
past. Sadly, a lot of people that go through
traumatic situations never let go and end up being
stuck in the past for the rest of their life. That is
why I wrote this book. I was the victim for a long
time. I allowed people to decide for me what I
could and could not do because I was the abused
child and everyone felt sorry for me. I played the
victim well too. Another thing about victims is
they have a difficult time forgiving and moving
forward. For a long time, I hated my mother for
leaving me. At least in my mind, that is what I
thought "My mother has abandoned me after
fighting so hard for me she just gave up" I would
discover later in life that was not the case.

As a military veteran and a police officer, I
have seen a lot of people play the role of the
victim. Over 17 years in law enforcement, I have

seen some crazy things. I have dealt with at-risk youth, college kids, and adults who all have played the role of a victim at some point or another. At some time in your life, you will experience the role of the victim. I have seen people blame their circumstances, lack of money, lack of social status, race, gender, sexual orientation and many other off the chart excuses of why they could not let go of their past and they chose to stay the victim. There are those that get out of the victim state at some point. For me, that came when I went into the military. I said to myself "Sean it is time to let it go, man"! "What is done is done and you have no control over it"! I became the survivor. I had gone through some very traumatic things but I had overcome them or at least I thought I did.

The survivor was the next step for me. The survivor believes they have really let go and moved forward but they have not. One of the biggest reasons is because they have a hard time forgiving themselves for going through the situation. The survivor will attempt to move forward but every time they try to move forward, they run into fear and hesitation and it holds them back. The survivor really thinks they are okay until they are set off by the slightest trigger that forces them to go back to their past and slip back into the victim role. I realize now, I did this many times between my time in foster care, the military, and during my first marriage. Many times I started out the survivor but fell back into the victim role. The reason this happened was because in my mind I had let the past go, but in my heart it was a different story. Then I became a winner.

The winner is what I want to help everyone who reads this book strive to be. No matter what has happened you deserve to be a winner. Winners take adversity and they deal with it, accept it, learn from it, and leave it. A winner is willing to truly let go and forgive the act. The winner is willing to peel back the onion and look at all the layers of the situation. Winners recognize the triggers, acknowledge them, don't let them affect them, and then keep moving forward. Most importantly winners recognize it is not enough to survive.

You can be in a gun battle get shot up and survive but you're in a wheelchair the rest of your life. You can be abused mentally and physically and survive but live in fear the rest of your life. You can fail at something and never try again. Get the picture here? Just because you survive does not mean that you won. The winners recognize this and understand it is not about surviving it is about winning.

My transition from just being a survivor to becoming a winner began with meeting my beautiful wife Lynn. Lynn helped me to find God. Through God and only God, I was able to discover what was holding me back at the age of 32. It was the simple fact I had not forgiven my mother. Now the survivor in me had forgiven her in my mind but my heart had not let go. It was not until God spoke to me at a retreat through scripture that I discovered the healing process I needed.

Colossians 3: 12-13 says-

Put on then, as God's chosen ones, holy and beloved, compassionate hearts, kindness, humility, meekness, and patience, bearing with one another and, if one has a complaint against another, forgiving each other; as the Lord has forgiven you, so you also must forgive.

It was when I read this that I realized what I had to do. Forgiving my mother was the beginning to really becoming a winner of my life. I was no longer just surviving and pretending like I had let it go. I accepted the truth. My mother never abandoned me. She saved my life by putting me into the foster care system and she sacrificed our relationship and stayed with Thomas living in fear for the next 20 plus years and taking on massive mental and physical abuse. I am proud to say my mother is a winner now and she has been able to get her life back and live out the rest of her years in peace.

No longer the victim or the survivor, God helped me see how to become a winner and now I want to help others do the same thing. In the next part of this book, I am going to welcome you to an 8 step M.O.V.E.M.E.N.T. process. I believe everyone deserves to be a winner. Unfortunately, not everyone will become one because they get stuck being a victim their whole life or they become a survivor but slip back into the victim role every time life gets a bit challenging. Today is the day you start winning.

Chapter 4

The Movement Process

Movement is an acronym. Each letter in the word introduces a new step. The 8 step Movement process focuses on Mindset, Opportunity, Vision, Empowerment, Momentum, Education, Navigation and Transformation.

The cool part about the Movement process is that you can start from the beginning or get in where you fit in. I am going to give you a brief overview because in the future year I will be writing in depth about each individual step with expert interviews, success stories, and strategies to help you gain the right movement in your life. In order to create movement, you must first learn how to move. In this chapter, we are going to focus on how to begin to let go of your adversity and move forward with your life.

1. Mindset

Mindset focuses on the way you think and feel about your life. The way you think and feel about things in your life will attract what you get in life. This is also known as the law of attraction or as I like to call it faith. Mindset is the anchor for everything else in the Movement program. Without the right mindset, you can't create Movement.

I remember when I went into foster care my mindset was a fixed one. I had been hurt, I was confused, and I felt abandoned by the one person I thought loved me more than life itself and would never choose anyone else over me. I did not have any clue how to overcome the pain inside of me. For years this was a major obstacle in my life and even though I tried to hide it inside my emotional core, I was still dealing with it.

There are two different types of mindset. A fixed mindset that focuses on what you learn and adopt into your life. People with a fixed mindset can only get so far in their life because they learn something, adopt and implement it, and accept that is as good as it gets. A lot of a fixed mindset is based on the way you were raised, educated, and the challenges you had to go through.

A growth mindset allows you to take what you have learned, apply it, and then be open to learning more. When you are open to learning more, you increase your personal value. You are coming up with more ways to deal with challenges and open up your mind to bigger things than just what you see in front of you. By creating a growth mindset you will not only be in a better position to deal with things in your life that have happened, you will also be able to recognize things before they happen that could have a negative impact in your life.

To really grow and develop a growth mindset, you must be willing to work on your mindset every day. There are lots of cool things you can do daily. For example, read books, watch videos, meditate, and implement personal development time that enhances growth and curiosity.

Things you can do to improve your mindset over time include:

Positive thinking as much as possible. Chances are you have faced some serious adversity in your life and you may still be trying to figure out how to deal with it. It all starts with your mindset. A positive mindset is the start point to get out of the dark and find the light again in your life. This does not happen overnight either. It took me 22 years to recognize this and another 11 years to gain clarity on exactly what it was I did to get out of it. I learned through other people's genuineness and kindness that I could move forward and I realized the more positive my thinking was the more blessed and free I became.

Focus on what you can control and not what you can't. When something bad happens to you there are only a few options. You can let it take control and dominate your life or you can address it without letting it conquer you. When I got out of the abusive situation I had the option of just accepting everything I had been told was true and

I would amount to nothing and be nothing the rest of my life or I could learn from the situation and let go of it and move forward towards an amazing life I could not physically see but I knew it was possible. I made a promise to myself I would be a good husband and father and I would never allow my family to live a life like I had as a child. I knew I could control that. I learned from my adversity that I could not control and grew from it. When my first son was born it was an easy decision to let go of the military and pursuit my law enforcement career so I could be in his life.

Another resource that really helped me was changing my circle of influence. When I surrounded myself with genuine positive minded people my life began to change. When I met my second wife Lynn. She showed me how God loved me for all my flaws. Her family accepted my son and me and made us a part of something really special. This boosted my confidence and increased my thirst for knowledge to know more about God and how he could change my life so I could be a better man, father, and husband.

One more thing that really helped was focusing on my personal health. When I ate right, got good sleep, and exercised my mind was full of oxygen and opened to learning and growing more. The better you feel the stronger your mindset will become. The goal is to feel a little bit better every day even in the most challenging times. If you want to serve and help others you must first master serving and helping yourself. It all starts with your personal health.

2. Opportunity

In order to get out of a bad situation, you must be open to finding new opportunities. Opportunity is the next step. If you have a growth mindset this will be really easy. If you are stuck in a fixed mindset the opportunities will come but you will miss them. I want to make sure you don't miss any opportunities so do not skip the mindset development step.

If you are in the right growth mindset the opportunities will come. You will see with clarity these opportunities and they will come in many forms. When you have a positive outlook you will attract positive things into your life. This is easier said than done because bad things happen in your life. You can't just put on your red slippers and click your heels three times and make everything okay. It takes time to attract the things you want into your life but there are ways to accelerate the process. There are lots of books and videos that share how to do this. One of the best books I discovered was Think and Grow Rich by Napoleon Hill. Napoleon Hill studied all of the successful men of his time and discovered unique qualities they all shared. One of the biggest ones was always thinking in a positive way.

Start thinking bigger than where you are at and trust your intuition. There are so many opportunities waiting for you. Just because you cannot see them yet does not mean that they are not there. Sometimes we are too set on what is within our grasp. We want that because we can see it. We do not have the vision to see past it to the even bigger opportunities that are just a bit out of reach but are coming our way.

71

Some people will be worried about if the opportunity is right or not. I say trust your gut instinct. As a police officer, I learned to trust my instincts daily to stay safe and go home every night. We all have the capability of doing this. Think of it like your spider sense. Your spider sense will tell you when an opportunity is right and not right. In order to get out of a bad situation, you must be open to new opportunity that comes your way.

3. Vision

People will tell you all the time what they want. How many conversations have you been a part of where you were engaged in a conversation and the people you were talking to kept saying what they wanted to have? Maybe it was you telling someone what you want to have. This is the first step to vision.

It is important to implement the idea of what you want but what if you really want to have it? This is where the rubber meets the road and a lot of people are not willing to go any further than the idea. Go back and look at successful people in your life and outside of your life. Most of them went through hell to get to the other side taking massive action. What does that mean for you? You can do the same thing.

Here is a really cool vision strategy for you. Visualize what you want. Write it down. Start to visualize every day that you already have it. Imagine how your life is different now. Every day pray and visualize this life over and over again. The more you do this the more God will bring the opportunities to you to make it happen. Let me be clear you will have to take action and seize the moment when the opportunities come your way.

You must be willing to see something, believe with all your heart you will have it, and then seize the opportunity and take the action to get it. Now do you see how the first three components have to work together in order for this to work? With the right mindset, you attract the right opportunities. The right opportunities allow you to visualize what you want and the action allows you to get it.

4. Empowerment

The last part of learning to move is to become empowered. The more you implement the first three steps the easier the fourth will come. It will come out of nowhere because you have a positive attitude, you are finding the right opportunities, and you are visualizing and taking action to see results. This leads right into feeling empowered.

When you become empowered you will have the confidence and strength of a lion to do anything you want to do. The bonus to this is the more empowered you become the more you will move. Once you start to move then you can focus on creating movement.

Here is how you can move your adversity into the right opportunity. First, focus on the mindset. What are your thoughts? Are you looking for the silver linings or allowing the dark clouds to hang over you? Once your mindset is right you will start to see the difference in your life. You will recognize opportunities that are right for you. Then you start to visualize what your life will be like when you take action on your opportunities. What does your life look like now? What will it look like in the future? Finally, you will become empowered to accomplish these goals because you will begin to feel good. You will recognize what you can and cannot control and reduce the stress. Finally, you will be strong and confident each day that you continue to apply this strategy in your life.

Remember you must learn how to move before you start creating movement. Understanding the power of a strong growth mindset, being open to exploring opportunities, creating powerful vision, and being empowered to move forward are the first four fundamentals to learn. Now that you know how to move it's time to create Movement. Are you ready?

Chapter 5
Time to Create Movement

Now that you know how to move it's time to move forward. The next step towards doing that is building momentum. Momentum is what keeps energy going. Momentum is the quantity of movement you have. When you start to move you have to keep moving. With the right momentum, you can do it. In order to create the momentum, you must have the first 4 steps down and working. If any of them are off even just a bit it can throw off your momentum.

I learned a lot about momentum when I enlisted in the Army. For the first several months there was somebody there guiding me, mentoring me, and motivating me to move. The drill sergeants would say move your butt Private Wyman. One of my favorite lines in basic training was "your moving like pond water". In Ranger School, it was all about movement. Tactical movement to avoid detection from the enemy. Quick movement to gain advantage and negotiate terrain to gain time to eat and sleep. Movement to make decisions and take action.

Momentum is action and action is needed to gain continuous motion. When you take action you automatically begin to build momentum. I have had the honor of working with some amazing people in my life. One thing all successful people do is take action steps every day. Even if you only take one step a day, you will be one step closer to crushing your adversity and opening up new doors to success.

Next, we are going to discuss education. Knowledge is power. Having a strong desire to learn will help you so much. First when you learn something new you create value within yourself. When you create value in yourself you are more valuable to others. Personal value is important and the best way is to always focus on investing in yourself mentally, physically, spiritually, and financially. You should always be striving to learn something new.

One of the most important things to learn is how to communicate. A year ago I partnered with a friend of mine in Canada. He was one of the top speakers in the world and he offered to mentor me. Starting out a year prior as a speaker I had some success but I knew I was capable of more. I started working with my mentor. I kept an open mind and was willing to learn everything he was willing to offer to me.

My mind was like a sponge learning about the professional speaking industry, learning how to become a great speaker with strong stage presence, discovering the foundation of business coaching, and learning the principles of selling. What I discovered was communication was the key to success. That is for another book though. The main point here is no matter what you think you know you can learn more if you are open to learning it. Always keep your mind open to learning and growing every day.

The next step in the movement process is going to focus on Navigation. No matter where you are in life right now you have to start somewhere. Some of you will realize you are right where you started from, while others recognize there has been some movement but not as much as you like, and then there will be others that are moving but they don't really have a road map. No matter where you are the first step is to identify where you are right now.

In the military and law enforcement, I had to learn how to navigate. If I did not know where I was going I could not accomplish my mission or answer my calls. As a field training officer, one of the biggest challenges was watching new police officers struggle with navigation. A high priority call would go out and the rookie officer would just take off. After we would get going lights and sirens I would ask them "where are you going?" They would turn and look at me with the deer in the headlights look and say I am not sure! I would calmly tell them to pull over and find out where we are going. Now I could have told them where to go but in the end that would not help them learn how to navigate and get from their start point to their final destination. This is a mission critical skill for police officers. If we do not know where we are going we cannot get to the scene to protect and serve.

A great scripture I learned and apply every day is Proverbs 4:26 which talks about carefully considering the path for your feet so all your ways can be established. If you do not know where you are going in your life then you can never reach your destination. By finding the right path to follow and staying true to that path you will be able to reach your destination.

Wouldn't it be great to set a start point and an end point and just go and get there? The problem is there are these things called obstacles that can get in our way. Now if you have learned how to move correctly, have built up momentum, and are constantly learning and growing it will be difficult for obstacles to stop you but there is one obstacle that can stop you dead in your tracks. It's called fear.

"The thing you fear most has no power. Your fear of it is what has the power. Facing the truth really will set you free." -Oprah Winfrey

There is a four letter word that makes people quit, give up and lose hope. Fear has a way of settling into people's heads and dominating their thought process. You must face your fears head on. Fear is the biggest reason why most people never get started striving towards their goals. People will forever say what they want. They will pump themselves up and proclaim, "I am going to do it!" Then this little voice in their head pops up and says, "But what if you don't? What if you can't? I have encountered this little voice more times than I would like to acknowledge, but I learned how to silence it.

You have to learn to face your fear head on. I call it turning your fear into fuel. If you're going to speak up about something, and that voice comes in your head, the only way to win is to speak. If you're going to do something big and that little voice crops up in your head, then you have to face it and do something big. If you don't, then fear will control you. This was a huge challenge for me. I grew up being told I would not amount to anything. Once I was even told that my mother would come home and I would be buried in the back yard.

I met fear many times being mentally and physically abused, bullied, divorced, my time in the military, and as a police officer working on the street. I know fear very well. The question you have to ask yourself is what are you afraid of? What is holding you back from letting go of your adversity and creating success?

As a law enforcement trainer, I have had the honor of training police officers and talking about fear a lot. What I discovered is fear is not a bad thing. I believe fear is a good thing because fear keeps you alert and focused which has kept me alive in many dangerous situations. The problem lies in allowing the fear to control you. When you let the fear overwhelm you and take control of your instincts and your emotions then you are in trouble.

I have had the honor of meeting some very heroic people in law enforcement. I have had a lot of police friends that have been involved in shootings and I have heard their stories. Sadly, I have gone to a lot of law enforcement funerals as well where officers made the ultimate sacrifice. As a law enforcement trainer, one of my jobs was to learn what keeps police alive and going home. As I studied and researched more and more I discovered the people that survived the traumatic incidents were able to identify their fear and manage it during the crisis. No matter what obstacles you face as long as you are moving with momentum, you can get around them or go right through them in a very short period of time.

For a long time fear had a psychological advantage over me. The reason my stepfather was able to be so successful at controlling my mother and I was because he knew how to intimidate and manipulate us using fear. As I got older I discovered fear was not so much physical as it was emotional. "False evidence appearing real". What I discovered next helped me turn my fear into fuel. Understanding that fear was what I was feeling emotionally and not physically allowed me to have control over it and turn it into fuel.

Joshua 1:9 Shares a great scripture about fear.

God commands us to be courageous and strong. Do not be afraid or discouraged, for the lord your God is with you everywhere you go. With him by your side there is nothing to fear.

Chapter 6

Movement Transformation

The last part of the Movement Process is transformation. The transformation in your life will begin to naturally happen as you go through the movement process. In order to reach a true transformation, you must first learn how to move by creating a growth mindset, seeking out the right opportunities, creating the vision to succeed in the opportunities, and becoming empowered to take action. Once you start to move you will create momentum. Remember the more action you take the more momentum you will build. Next, you must be open to learning and educating yourself. Reading books, going to classes, investing in yourself in motivational and personal development seminars can all help to increase your knowledge base. Knowledge is power and it leads to confidence.

Next, you have navigation. Start with your start point then look at your end point. The shortest distance between two points is a straight line. If only it was that easy. You will face obstacles the biggest one will be the battle between your ears and being willing to face your fears.

If you are willing to do all these things on a consistent basis. You will begin to see the transformation. You will feel better. You will have more confidence. You will take action and no matter what adversity you have faced or will face you will have the right strategy to prepare and deal with anything that comes your way.

I believe everyone should transform their life into the one they truly want to have. The problem is most people do not know about this process. They go through life taking little risk, running from fear, and avoiding challenges that come along. I know this from experience. It took me too long to figure out how to get my head and my heart in the right place. It was not until I started following the 8 steps that I shared with you that I discovered how to create movement and move forward and finally let go of the anger and hate I had in my heart.

If you're in a situation right now where you feel stuck and want to get out but don't know how, I would like to connect with you. Look, reading this book and taking no action will be a waste of the investment you made to purchase it. I want to give you a massive return on your investment. I have an eight-week program to help you step by step work through this process. You will meet other people like you who are ready to move forward and together we will focus on creating the movement you need to move forward with your life.

For more information, contact me directly at **successwithseanwyman@gmail.com** to set up an exclusive exploration session to see if the program is right for you. The group is going to be limited to no more than 10 people at a time to make sure I can give 100% of my time and energy to helping you and connecting with you resources to eliminate your adversity and find your success.

I am also currently booking dates with high schools, colleges, universities, military personnel both active and veterans, law enforcement agencies and academies, at risk youth organizations, domestic violence organizations, and other non-profit organizations to share this process to help as many people as I can. To learn more go to:

http://www.successwithseanwyman.com/contact-sean-wyman/ before availability runs out.

Chapter 7

My Gift to You

Thank you for taking the time to read this book. I would like to close it out with a gift. The power of prayer has been so helpful during the most challenging times in my life. As a special thank you, I would like to pray for you.

God thank you for allowing me to be the vehicle to share this process with people in pain and stuck in adversity. I ask that you will open the hearts and minds of all who read this book to take action to create movement in their life. As you showed me God, everyone has a purpose and I know through your intervention this book will serve as a way to help people release their adversity and be open to the success you have to offer them. God you have proven, through you anyone can let go of their pain, anger, contempt, and fear and keep moving forward. Finally, I thank you God for all the adversity you made me face and the strength and courage that came from all of it including learning how to forgive, to move forward in my life even when I did not want to, and write this book through your guidance to serve others and show them there is a way out of their self-doubt and fear through you. I ask that you offer the same process to all who read this book so they can let go of their past trials and tribulations and move forward to have the life they deserve. To you goes all the glory. Amen.

Remember, when you are at your lowest is when you have the best opportunity to reach your greatness. Be willing to let go and follow the

Movement Process to the end. I look forward to seeing your transformation!

About Sean Wyman

Proverbs 4:26 says "Give careful thought to the path for your feet, and be steadfast in all your ways." These are words that Sean Wyman has learned to live by!

Sean Wyman is a Motivational Speaker, Certified Business Coach, Senior Marketing Strategist, Self-published Author, 8-year military Airborne Ranger Veteran, and a 17-year Law Enforcement Professional and Trainer.

He believes it is inside of all of us to live the life we want to live. From an abusive childhood, a near death experience in the Army, failing in his first marriage, and failing miserably for his first years getting started in business.

Sean shares how through God he turned each adversity into a life changing opportunity to help others not make the same mistakes in their life.

Sean's passion is helping people take action to create movement in their life as they make challenging decisions, crush adversity, eliminate self-doubt and keep moving forward.

Discover Great Bulk Purchasing Options and Bring More Funding Into Your Organization

Ask Me How @

successwithseanwyman@gmail.com

Made in the USA
Lexington, KY
22 July 2017